Sylvan Grove

Barbara A. Meier

A Publication of The Poetry Box®

Editing, Book & Cover Design: Shawn Aveningo Sanders
Cover Photograph: Joan Detmer (joansphotostudio.com)

ISBN: 978-1-948461-80-1
Printed in the United States of America.
Wholesale Distribution via Ingram.

Published by The Poetry Box®, 2021
Portland, Oregon
ThePoetryBox.com

Dedicated to my mom, Rosella, the last surviving child of Henry and Margarethe Bentrup, Sylvan Grove, KS, and my Dad, Rudy Meier, who died much too young from ALS.

I would not be here today if my great-great-grandparents, great grandparents, and grandparents would not have homesteaded and lived on the prairies.

All I am has been shaped by them, just as the limestone was shaped by an ancient ocean and the fenceposts were quarried with an auger, plug, and feather.

Contents

"To be ignorant of what occurred before you were born is to remain always a child. For what is the worth of human life, unless it is woven into the life of our ancestors by the records of history?"

—Marcus Tullius Cicero

Sylvan Grove

The temporal
eternity.
Stones lie
in their beds of
grass. The grass
slowly bends
West.
Grey
marble heads, the trees
twisted where storms
sought shelter.
The prairie
ascends, slowly bends
up the slopes,
transfixed at the headstones.
A silent prayer of the prairie,
so temporal, it is
nothing else but
eternity itself, a life
too short to know.

Old Hi-Way 18

Grinding down old highway 18,
Sweat glues my chubby thighs
to black cracked vinyl and my sister's thigh.
The knob of the gear shift between my legs,
These are the rusty roads on maps in my brain.

Memories like a 3D Google map
of a cottonwood tree, a ditch with muddy water,
rescuing ladybugs...

The stories I remember—
I wrap in newsprint, white and black,
to cushion from falls from rock quarries
I excavate from a prefrontal trap
in the SW corner, smack
dab in the cerebellum.

They rest in corrugated boxes,
stacked like hay bales in the back
of a dusty blue Ford pickup,
Paradoxes wrapped in twine and baling wire.

The Electric Fence

The wheat, radiant rays to the sun,
dazzles our eyes in a Klimt* shower of gold.
Grasshoppers play dodgeball with our sunburnt bodies,
fwipping the air with their wings.
We laugh at the dog - the sentinel dog,
jumping so high to see the way over chin high walls of wheat.
The horizontal landmarks: tree, fence post, wire.
The tree to catch the clouds,
the fencepost to nail down the grass,
the wire to conduct electricity.
All to keep us and the cows in the field..

We'd march militant into the rows of wheat,
keeping time with hidden cicadas.
Southward to the border, field rimmed and wired,
grounded in a metal pole with porcelain earrings.
A silver strand, a spider's bite humming in its veins.
The wire forbidden.

"Did Daddy really say?"

"Would it really...?"

We reached to grasp the silver line,
whispering in the silence.
We felt the bite, disobeyed our dad.

Years later our daddy dead, the sentinel dog a ghost
between the stalks of wheat, and the fence corroded,
I remember the disobedience of death in a father's words,
and now know the obedience of a son
to take the sting of electric fences.

The Garden of Eden

The gate to Eden is really only barb wire fencing
strung between crook-necked sticks,
hinged to rust-streaked limestone posts, bleeding on the prairie.
A gate to keep the pasture in place for children and cows;
to play among devil's claw, sucking the dirt
from the roots of wild onions with purple flowers,
or play hide and seek with horny toads and box turtles.
At its tightest, saggy trousers and tattered shirts,
the latch, a belt of baling wire slick in my sweaty palms.
Open, it flops in a hopscotch trap,
with barbs of steel poking the ground.
We were sentinels of silage,
hauled in a dying farmer's Ford pickup.
Prairie angels with sunflower swords, keeping out all that is bad—
escaping the wrath of rattlesnakes, fire ants, and sand burrs.
The Garden of Eden, before the fall.

The Sunshine of Beer

There is sunshine in the taste of beer:
of a June wheat day, blonde grain kissing
the cerealan blue sky, and a 103 temperature
baking the green enamel of a John Deere 55 H combine.

It is the smell of bread brewing on the prairie wind.
The farmer, cabless with his Coors,
babysitting his girls in the bin of the combine,
perched above the churning gears.

There were so many ways to die that day:
in the jaws of the combine, sliding on
cracked vinyl seats without a seatbelt,
riding the tipping truck, dumping wheat
at the grain elevator, hoping the elevator man
would give us a stick of gum.

OSHA* never knew and KCSL* never cared
about us sipping the last swallow of daddy's beer.
They never knew it was the farmer who died.

Was it the pink mercury treated wheat in the old JD seed drill?
The Barban (carbyne) for the wild oats? Or was it the visit
to Sasebo, Japan, swabbing the deck of radiation?

Death blooms from the seeds
drilled into the ground so long ago.
We are harvested by the deed done wrong,
the accidents unknown, the ignorance of greed.
We become the brewed amber ale drunk down.

Jerusalem Upon the Plain

The radiance is of wheatfields
fed to the craw of a John Deere combine.
The green against the gold
honeyed fields and milky blue skies.
The hills outside my car window roll westward,
flattening to shorn stubbled fields
and shaggy carpets of bluestem, buffalo, and switchgrass.
The tedium of our wheels on Interstate 70—
Sylvan Grove, Ellsworth, Russell, Victoria, Hays.
My eyes sink, fade to my cheek, resting against the hot glass:

I contemplate…
What bliss can be found in the plainness of the high prairie?
What pastures of the sick shine with a glorious sheen?

The halls of Zion
in the basement of Hadley hospital
where martyrs sleep in hospital beds,
and sticky peanut butter girls behind urine green bathroom stalls
belt angel songs- funneling through heating ducts
conjubilant with song
a feast to shout among the ailing throng.
It is "A blessed country sweet in death, a home to the elect."
Our song of triumph resounds
'round floors, 'neath beds, through IVs,
in comas, and last breaths.
It is Jerusalem upon the Plains—
a throne of golden wheat, and milk and honeyed earth,
The conquerors faithfully brought to rest upon the Armo plains.
Blood of earth and heaven pumping through our veins.
We are little girls clothed in robes of white.

Building with Post Rock Limestone

The compression of the Kansas sea laid layers
of dead extinct creatures inches below, softly molded
to layers of earth, the overburden peeled back
like so much dead skin; a seam of solidified bone.
Just as the seam was laid so the father laid the fence posts.
The man laboring in veins with an auger, plug, and feather,
dragging posts on wishbone sleds, tipping, tamping,
stringing with wire. He built his family upon the plains.
The weight of rock bending his back
in the years of children and grandchildren.

We, too, can excavate the limestone rock,
with drill, plug, and feather, like our father.
We, who are children of the plains.
Heavy memories solidifying when exposed to air.
We tip and tamp our lives, layering
the bones in seams of years.
We who remain, honor his name
and labor not in vain.

On a Tornado Warning in Emporia, KS

I cannot walk out of the atmospheric river
by myself, especially at 5:00 PM when the wind
shifts bringing the charnel smell of a slaughterhouse
with cauterized blood: a miasma of death,
tinting the skies coppery with bruising green clouds.
White sunlight being scattered by marble size hail.
The clouds hiss, and boil like a snake curling down to strike.
A dry line encounter: where moist meets dry.
The passion for death in a dance of wind:
culminating in a 2x4 impaled in a tree.

Death is the only outcome of this storm.
And at that moment when it jumps from the north,
I see it spawning little devils on the horizon…
Mocking me in a brief grim dance.
Toe to earth and then back up to heaven.

It is finished.

In the silence after the storm…
The breath comforts me, gently calls my name
and I realize the relief of birds chirping in a fallen creation.
This little resurrection gives life
to the destruction and debris that is my life.
The blood not burnt the body not charred,
the water a rain of grace-colors refracting
rainbow lights in an atmospheric river.

Tornado

When white sunlight
hits hail scatters
the narrow beams
of light,
they plank the sky
in hues of eerie yellow.

Ping-
ponging
off each other—
a game of pinball,
igniting lights
with each slam.

In that engulfing gloom,
the bruised sky,
full of broken veins
of light,
pool
into violently spinning air.

The fat finger of death
curls its way to dirt—
wedging itself downward.

Mesmerized
By power flashes,
I strain to glimpse
The finger of God.

In that frozen
moment—
thoughts on the internet
waves,
Doppler Radar
pinging velocity
across the plains,
I see where the blue turns to black,
and roars to silence.

The neutrality of Space,
inert,
a vacuum
that is you.

I am gravity,
spiraling earthward—
an ice ball,
burning up
in atmospheric divergence.

Face planted to fears,
grounded in a crater
of my own making.

In your silence, I stand...
watching the approaching supercell.
It surges forward in the darkness,
wrapped in rain,
cloaked
from sight.

I await the ending—
the surrender,
debris swirling
to the West,
My pieces—
scattered—
landing in someone's front yard…

Wild Uncle Bill's Sword

A sword, Cavalry born,
buried in silver strands of buffalo grass.
Fallen, from a running soldier's hand,
face down, in a rutted gully.
A man of Custer's 7th Cavalry
his blood rusted in prairie dirt, forgotten by time,
found by a wayward sheepherder:
Wild Uncle Bill's sword.
We too are the dead on the prairie.
Our bodies bleed out, cradled
in the soft embrace of greasy grass.
We are the sheep upon the hill,
stumbling over half-buried
swords and artifacts of ancient battles.
Losing ourselves in canyon brush, for juicy bits,
we spy over the hill. We are the ones
the shepherd breaks to keep us from ourselves.

A Creature from the Black Lagoon

The current knots the sodden weeds, brushing
ankles. Twining memories of lagoon
brackish creature, opal eyed, fins of blushing
mohawk feathers. Death swims naked in moon
shadows, stroking thighs with whispery nails,
leaving trace beneath horny-webbed claws;
Tapetum lucidum, crystal-like veils,
Adam's DNA, sin of blame, the flaw.
Tears hide at the eye's sharp corners.
Sorrow reveals the creases, buried
adipocere. The dead and mourners
gathered like weeds, submerged and ferried,
rising like bubbles to the pool of blood,
We are drowning, anchored in clay and mud.

A Rag Rug

So that's that …
The end of the fabric—
the string run out,
the garment created,
unraveling …

A frayed shirt,
ripped in Grandma's blind hands.

No words:
without weave,
or a thread
of respect, or honor,
for the ending hem.

Just the rip in a pink and orange culotte skirt traveling to the rag bag …

The silence,
broken by the one and a half-inch snip,
lengthwise, to start the tear.
The rasp of my fury,
your hellish silence.
I am scorned,
hooked in a crochet braid,
stitched in a spiral,
laid upon the floor.

Abilene: First Night Home

Strike the old set.
Replace those earth-clinging trees.
Remove the ocean's breath.
Thin out the mountains in the sky.
Tune out Interstate 5.
Change the scene to:
Hot, dry heat, a prairie sigh.
a windmill creaking, groaning
under the weight of night.
Offset it with coyotes howling
and an overture of nocturnal insects,
add the clatter of a feeder, a bawling calf.
I enter, the extras offstage, carrying
on about harvest and baby Sarah.
I move downstage to face the horizon,
huge and uncluttered. The stars
come on as lights on a stage.

The solo spot, the moon
in its yellowish-orange glory,
focuses on me and home.

Lightning Bugs

In August the shooting stars melt across the sky
like so many lightning bugs in June
in glass Ball jars.

The shooting star heat,
radiates outward from the center,
beating against the glass walls,

like the kitchen humming
in freezer notes, with yellow pools
of light dangling from a string.

We are late-night bakers,
on a prairie train
bound for nowhere...

The memory of you,
like the lightning bugs and stars
found dead at the bottom of the jar in the morning.

Bas Relief

The marble played freeze tag
across the plaza.
The evening breeze brought Greece to mind,
while General Motors lost its way
in Kansas City.

A roller skater on an Olympian run
passed our table. We laughed
as we thought of skates on gravel.

The ice melted in the gin.
Evening fell in among us,
kept us company:
a marbled night in bas relief.
Conversation froze around us,
marble browned in the cracks,
the ruins enough for me.

The Dying Gaul

The body sprawls in sleep. Sheets like crumpled paper
cover the marble limbs, while the pillow smothers
the sounds of morning birds outside the bedroom window.

This effigy of a man sharing my bed, a dying warrior
resting on his shield in sacrificial exhaustion,
la petite mort, he stirs not, as I study the form
and the curve of his body 'neath the sheet.

In the chill of dawn, I seek the warmth of him one last time
before the line between our bodies separates
and the bedsprings can't hold. The frame falls apart.
Remembering can't hold you next to me
or stop the wound from bleeding on your chest.

Complin

Under a blanket of prairie grasses,
beneath a thunder moon, masses
of Lampyridae play tag with lover's hands.
A night smothered in tinny sounds and bands
of cicadas, the clang of pig feeders, windmill vanes
creaking in a shifting breeze. The rain
of June stars splatters on your skin.
It is completion, an evening complin.

I trace from lip to alabaster neck,
the line made straight, despite the body wrecked.
With my lips, I can burn my words
into your flesh, a brand light as a bird's
wing, feathering your shoulder, a shadow
at night I can only see. A tableau
of a prairie night, the moon, man, and me.

The Eastern Boxelder Bug:
Boisea Trivittata

Boxelder bugs bask among the yellow cream stone,
sucking up the warmth from the dead bodies embedded
in the Greenhorn limestone formation. The Boisea Trivittata:
redbanded, scented, and promiscuous. Carrying and pulling
to-and-fro. Anonymous sex among the ruins of a Cretaceous Sea.

Swarming in October seeking shelter in rock crevices,
living life in sleep till the sun bakes the southern wall in spring.

We too could seek shelter in cracks of rock walls.
formed by the hairline kiss becoming the breached cavity
permeable by the sweaty sheen of our summer bodies.
The tension stronger than the strength of us, spalling cracks
and crumbling stone. We are the brittle failure.

Our lives in bug language, multiple mates, dragging each other
to-and-fro. Love among the Eastern boxelder bugs.

Dedicated to the SE Section 34, Township 43-N, Range 19-W

inspired by William Carlos William

Of this plot of ground,
facing Haw Creek,
the steadfast stones
in the family cemetery
the hum of the vestiges
of lives lived on the prairie.

Of Valaria Ernestine Wacker
who told her granddaughter
of a story about bushwhackers
and raids on a farm in Missouri.
A dour woman,
a preacher's daughter,
never smiling, speaking
with German in her voice

the story told by her grandmother to her.

Of Wilhamine Caroline Tagtmeyer,
who married in 1863,
in Cole Camp, Missouri,
and lived on a farm,
in Morgan County Missouri,
cattywampus from Little Dixie,
and next door to Benton County,

Of ruffians on horses, searching for whatever,
wearing their fancy embroidered shirts with long hair blowing

[. . .]

on fast rides and dismounts as they burned the barns,
raided the smokehouses, upending tables,
slashing furniture with cavalry swords,
storming a bedroom to flip the mattress for money or gold,
not seeing the baby asleep on top the patchwork quilt
of greens, blues, browns and rusty reds.

Of the heart of a mother fearing the silence.
Of saving the baby from a feather mattress soft in its suffocation
or to wait to watch the plunging sword, rip the feathers
into a drift of bloody plumes
The sounds of stomping boots, trailing flour and coffee,
killing the cattle for supper.

It was the civil war, border ruffians, raids, and skirmishes
on the Fisher family farm in the southwest
quarter of the SE Section 34, Township 43-N
Range 19-W.

I wonder why she told this granddaughter
this story?

What I do know:

If you don't want to remember your grandmother's stories
your own memories don't count.

A Mother

The wheat soaks up the sun, green is turning to gold
with a sky in blue mourning, draping the hills
in a pall of brocade shot through with gold.

In the field, the hawk's warning pierces
the drum of a rodent's ear. The tall wheat
masks the mother scampering down
a dark tunnel with nesting straw.

Listen! The combine comes to mow down her world.
Run! Destruction is in the grinding gears and the chop
of descending blades. The straw laid crisp in windrows.

In the distance, lightning strikes the earth,
sending shock waves through the air in a sonic boom!
The crack of thunder expands with each bolt
giving way to a long low rumble: brontide.

Sarah, Rachael, and Hannah, too, heard the dull thunder,
pleaded nightly in a mother's voice, groaning and praying
for a baby and for the children lost to Bael and Herod,

just as the mother of scurrying rodents fear the hawk,
the blade, the sound. Hidden by straw-lined nests deep
underground,
they cannot stop the swarms of thunderstorms, swallowing

the sky, eating the earth with piercing talons, harvesting
wretchedness to be flung in their faces.
The human denial of birth, sad mothers cannot understand.

No mother can forget the soft smell of skin velvet,
buried in the crook of a child's neck.
The smother of tiny kisses wreck
their lives and suck the breath away.

Lives and Loves Lost in the Skeletons of a Limestone Structure

At the Opera House, the shadows march
militantly through the sunken Sokal gymnasium,
building "a strong mind in a strong body,"
dining on smoky air, from a spectral kitchen.

Above the basement, Blind Boone warms up the piano,
while the dancers in the ballroom flit and skim
the hardwood floors, inches above the sawdust.

They are wraiths to the audience,
ephemeral in history, transparently
strolling through the burnt-out shell
of the Opera house; the dancers, gymnasts,
and pianists boarding the Butterfield Overland
Express and the Kansas Union Pacific Railroad.

If I listen carefully, I can hear
the stagecoach rumble across the prairie,
and ragtime playing on the street.
At night I sleep with the ghosts at the Midland Railroad Hotel,
listening to the train, whistle and grumble,
grieving the nights and chattering through the day.
The Union Pacific fails to stop for the phantoms, crowding
the train tracks and the sidewalks in front of the Opera House.

We are all just sojourners here, residing with the revenants.

The Opera House

Turner Hall was built of Native limestone in 1901 in Wilson, Ks. It later became known as the Wilson Czech Opera House. The basement contained a gym, a kitchen, and a dining hall. On the first floor were a stage, a ballroom, and a balcony. Vaudeville acts performed in the early years. One such famous act was Blind Boone. Unfortunately, the Opera House burned down in 2009.

ragtime plays above
the stage, ghostly sojourners
the past- burnt sawdust

trains grumbling at night
stagecoaches rattle the plains
the prairie empties

Fragility

In the rusty patches of ripened sorghum
along Highway 18, west of Sylvan Grove
I can see the trail back home
under the forever sky

I stand solid like the limestone post-rock
at the corners of the fields, watching
the black Angus on the hills. At my
feet, the pasture gourds nestle against
the rubble from the roadcut

the barbed wire snags and draws blood
from my fragile skin of age
It's really not about the fragility
it's about the strength of the moment.

Naked Nymphs

Southwestern College, Winfield KS is a warm and exciting environment filled with students and alumni leading lives of significance.

> with lilac wreaths
> on goddess's hair
> bare-assed ladies run

The evening murmured with giggles, our scampering feet disturbing the bushes behind Smith Hall. Ghosts of students past watch with fascination the Olympic run down the gravel alley.

Gazing Out at the Walnut Valley, Remembering the 77 Steps at Southwestern College

~inspired by Richard Straw

I contemplate the steps, sitting on the wall, by Christy Hall.
The maple tree scarlet and the geraniums in baskets, Builder purple.

A spider rappels from tree to sidewalk crack
a deep canyon to trek, scurrying to the limestone wall.

forty years ago I roamed this college hill
never went back 'til now. I left alone.
I remain alone.

a web
between sunsets
in lilac bushes.

Reunion, 1979-2019

The milo rusts in the fields. Above, a hazy light
surrounds the blades of a turbine windmill,
creating a nimbus against the forever sky.

The clouds weep on the horizon
and I am on their path of tears,
filling memory pools on Interstate 70

An asphalt time tunnel rumbling across the prairie;
abandoning the farms, leaving limestone fence posts
leaning with saggy belts of barbwire
The pump jacks* bedded in the pastures,
rocking the cattle to sleep.

The grain elevators, crumpled metal
abandoned and discarded by the train tracks.
Not one engine slows as they barrel across
the High Plains, leaving towns mostly deserted,
just as my Subaru leaves no trace on I 70.

I left too, abandoning my life,
only to come back to the lie.
The regret of nodding donkeys*
with Kansas, lost and forsaken
in my rearview window.

"When stories are not told, they become something else.... forgotten."

—Tatiana de Rosnay, *Sarah's Key*

Notes

Sylvan Grove was founded in 1877, at the site where a mill had been built in 1875. The city was named for twin sylvan groves near the original town site. Sylvan Grove is located at 39°0′46″N 98°23′33″W (39.012860, -98.392491).

Dedication

Auger, plug, and feather refers to a technique for splitting stone using a three-piece toolset.

ALS: Amyotrophic Lateral Sclerosis.

"The Electric Fence"

Klimt as in Gustav Klimt, artist.

"The Sunshine of Beer"

OSHA: Occupational Safety and Health Administration.

KCSL: Kansas Children's Service League.

"Jerusalem Upon the Plain"

A blessed country sweet in death, a home to the elect and *clothed in robes of white* refers to the hymn "Jerusalem The Golden" by Bernard of Cluny, translated by J.M. Neale.

"Reunion: 1979-2019"

Pump jacks: overground drive for a reciprocating piston pump in an oil well.

Nodding donkeys: another name for a pumpjack.

Acknowledgments

Poems in this manuscript have appeared, some in slightly different form, in the following publications:

“The Electric Fence,” *Highland Parks Poetry Challenge* (2018)

“The Garden of Eden,” *Nature Writing* (2017)

“The Sunshine of Beer,” *Pure Slush* (2018)

“Jerusalem Upon the Plain,” *JONAH* (2017)

“Building with Post Rock Limestone,” *Lines and Stars* (2017)

“Tornado,” *Cacti Fur* (2015)

“Complin,” *Sum* (2018)

“Dedicated to the SE section 34, Township 43-N, Range 19 W,” *100 Lives* (Pure Slush, 2020)

“Gazing Out at the Walnut Valley, Remembering the 77 Steps at Southwestern College,” *Dark Forest* (Flying Ketchup Press, 2021)

“Reunion 1979-2019” (as “Interstate 70”), *Wrong Way Go Back* (Pure Slush, 2020)

Praise for Sylvan Grove

"When I visited Kansas to share the poetry of my father, someone told me "Kansas is a state unaccustomed to literary affection; but your father loved who we are." In that tradition of prairie patriotism, *Sylvan Grove* leaves no doubt this place can be loved with honest lyric skill. The poems in this book return to iconic moments of perception in a landscape where miracles yield their bounty to the steady gaze. A guide to weather describes certain effects of light as *not rare, but rarely seen*, and this book brings to light myriad Edenic pleasures of Kansas ground. In the work of mending, turning sod, tornado watch, windmill, firefly, wheat turning green to gold, and other magic moments, Meier performs alchemy, turning the ordinary unseen to resonant glimpses that remain.

—Kim Stafford, author
Early Morning: Remembering My Father: William Stafford

"Barbara Meier spent her early childhood in a small Kansas town auspiciously named Sylvan Grove because its twin groves were a landmark in an otherwise almost treeless landscape. In twenty-six imagery-rich poems she invites us to attend her reunion with this place. We hear a calf bawling, the vanes of windmills clacking, cicadas. We feel the dangers of living on a farm: tornado supercells, chemicals, and the clashing of the combine's gears and blades when riding without a seat belt beside her father. Meier offers us the creatures of prairie from boxelder bugs to horny toads to the dying Ford pick-ups against a backdrop of her family's life. She includes stories from a family graveyard that a woman dare not forget if she is to know her place in this contemporary world of shifting horizons. I admire the juxtapositions in these poems of place—the limestone fenceposts of the north-central Kansas landscape, for example—with the sensitive and beautifully lyric spiritual and emotional connection to family, wheat fields, and the history buried in the soil both in the graveyard and in the fields where it was possible to find a sword from Custer's cavalry. William Stafford, one of Kansas' transplants to Oregon like Meier, became one of Oregon's finest poets. This Sylvan Grove work would be a collection he would have been drawn to— as was I.

—Tricia Knoll, author *of How I Learned to Be White*

"*Sylvan Grove* features a pleasantly surprising use of language, a delightful linguistic play in these poems, woven into an articulate and holistic world view. For the children in these poems, the "Garden of Eden" is a pasture in which they are *sentinels of silage... Prairie angels with sunflower swords.* But this is *Eden before the Fall,* and the farmer who owns these fields is dying among the many dangers and options for death among farm machinery, crops poisoned by unrecognized chemicals, and tornados spaw*ning little devils on the horizon...* In these pages, family lore on the prairie tells of *Wild Uncle Bill's Sword,* the rag rugs knotted by the grandmother's *blind hands,* and the *brittle failure* of mating rituals of Eastern boxelder bugs. There are echoes of William Stafford here, another poet whose myth-making began in Kansas and found its way to the Pacific Northwest. A quietly vivid debut.

—Carolyne Wright, author
This Dream the World: New & Selected Poems

"Readers of Barbara A. Meier's remarkable chapbook, *Sylvan Grove,* will quickly identify with its central theme: growing up in a precise geographical region, leaving, and then returning after a long absence.

With a keen eye and ear for lyrical imagery, Meier tells childhood stories about living on the Kansas plains where *We were sentinels of silage.../ Prairie angels with sunflower swords, keeping out all that is bad.../ The Garden of Eden, before the fall* ("The Garden of Eden"). These stories rest in *corrugated boxes,/ stacked like hay bales in the back/of a dusty blue Ford pickup,/ Paradoxes wrapped in twine and baling wire* ("Old Hi-Way 18").

When the poet returns home for the first time in forty years, the central paradox of this collection becomes clear: many things have changed except one: *I left alone./ I remain alone.* ("Reunion, 1979-2019"). This intimate—yet universal—truth must give us pause.

Meier knows what every good writer knows: a journey is not complete until its story is told. Readers will be grateful that she shares her journey and its stories in such engaging, vivid poetry. This is a collection not to be missed.

—Carolyn Martin, poetry editor,
Kosmos Quarterly: journal for global transformation

"Gorgeous and evocative, Meier's work is beautifully reminiscent without being sentimental. The poems in *Sylvan Grove* are resplendent with the countryside details of North Central Kansas, lines full of grasshoppers and barbwire, chest-high wheat and dogs leaping through the fields. I've been carrying these poems in my mind as I walk through my summer days, grateful for their imagery and precision. As you move through your day, these poems will stay with you.

—Peter Brown Hoffmeister, author of *Too Shattered for Mending*

"Barbara A. Meier's latest collection of poetry, *Sylvan Grove,* is not unlike any of her previous collections. There is a familiarity to her words and her passion for what she translates from eye to pen. It is both tactile and sensual. It is both accessible and intangible. And as much as that is comforting it is also deceiving. Because what lies beneath her words is a world of constant discovery and self-examination.

—Douglas Scott Delaney, author
Tower Dog: Life Inside the Deadliest Job in America
and *The Last Ten Miles of Avery J. Coping*

About the Author

Barbara A Meier traded an ocean of wheat for the Pacific Northwest in 1979. She married, had babies, and pretty much gave up on her dreams of acting and writing. Thirty-three years later, she found herself alone, staring at the Pacific Ocean, and writing poems again. She still wants to try and get back on stage.

Recently she retired from teaching kindergarten and moved to Colorado to spend time with her mom. She was just in time for the COVID-19 quarantine.

She has two chapbooks published *Wildfire LAL 6* (Ghost City Press, Summer 2019) and *Getting Through Gold Beach* (Writing Knights Press, November 2019). She has been published in *The Poeming Pigeon, TD; LR Catching Fire Anthology* and *The Fourth River.*

<https://basicallybarbmeier.wordpress.com>
<facebook.com/poetwholivedbythesea>

About The Poetry Box®

The Poetry Box® is a boutique publishing company in Portland, Oregon, who provides a platform for both established and emerging poets to share their words with the world through beautiful printed books and chapbooks.

Feel free to visit the online bookstore (thePoetryBox.com), where you'll find more titles including:

Nothing More to Lose by Carolyn Martin

Notes from a Caregiver by Meg Lindsay

Like the O in Hope by Jeanne Julian

A Shape of Sky by Cathy Cain

The Very Rich Hours by Gregory Loselle

Just the Girls by Pamela R. Anderson-Bartholet

Between States of Matter by Sherry Rind

The Kingdom of Birds by Joan Colby

Excoriation by Rebecca Smolen

My Mother Never Died Before by Marcia B. Loughran

Mouth Quill by Kaja Weeks

and more . . .

www.ingramcontent.com/pod-product-compliance
Ingram Content Group UK Ltd.
Pitfield, Milton Keynes, MK11 3LW, UK
UKHW040028200726
13854UKWH00001B/419

9 781948 461801